Raven perched on a jack pine

Text copyright © 2016 by Brian Heinz   Illustrations copyright © 2016 by Michael Rothman   Edited by Kate Riggs   Designed by Rita Marshall   Published in 2016 by Creative Editions
P.O. Box 227, Mankato, MN 56002 USA   Creative Editions is an imprint of The Creative Company   www.thecreativecompany.us

Library of Congress Cataloging-in-Publication Data   Names: Heinz, Brian. / Rothman, Michael.   Title: The Great North Woods / by Brian Heinz; illustrated by Michael Rothman.
Summary: In the northeastern region known as the Great North Woods, day dawns with quivering aspens, waters teem with life, forests prowl with predators, and nature is celebrated in rhyme.
Identifiers: LCCN 2015047477 / ISBN 978-1-56846-275-2   Subjects: CYAC: Stories in rhyme. / Nature—Fiction. / Forest animals—Fiction. / Forests and forestry—Fiction.
Classification: PZ8.3.H41344 Gr 2016 / 398.8—dc23   First edition 9 8 7 6 5 4 3 2 1

THE GREAT NORTH WOODS

Brian Heinz

illustrated by

Michael Rothman

Creative Editions

AT DAWN IN THE GREAT NORTH WOODS ...

Tricolored bumblebees and swamp thistle

Sunbeams chase the evening's chill
From moody forests, deep and still.
Aspens quiver in the breeze,
Thistles welcome bumblebees.
Pitcher plants crowd misty bogs
Of muck and mired rotting logs.

Bobcat stirring in his lair,
Preening, cleaning matted hair—
Rested, ready for a day
Of hunting unsuspecting prey.

Bobcat; northern pitcher plant; Sphagnum *mosses*

Great gray owl in a black spruce

Great gray owls fold their wings,
This is what the morning brings

At Dawn in the Great North Woods.

The trill of the loons, a rich cascade
Of notes that echo in the glade.

Herons snatch up polliwogs,
Stab at perch and leopard frogs.

Great blue heron with polliwog (tadpole)

12

Rafts of mallards, blue-winged teals,
Tip their bottoms, dip for meals.

Milfoil, duckweed, scuds, and grasses—
From bills to bellies, hunger passes.

Male and female mallards in water; blue-winged teal in flight

13

Anglers hail from near and far
In hopes of catching longnose gar.

Walleyes and bullheads cruise about
With rock bass and salmon and rainbow trout

In the Waters of the Great North Woods.

Longnose gar with water lilies

Walleye and black bullhead catfish

IN THE FORESTS OF THE GREAT NORTH WOODS ...

Gray wolves in a forest of black spruce

A pack of gray wolves trotting south,
Bristling fur and panting mouths.

A bull moose yearling's startled grunt
Signals the clan is on the hunt.
Excited howls are drawing near,
Spilling waves of mortal fear.
Bull moose races for the lake
And plunges in for safety's sake.

Shoulder deep, he turns around
To face his foes and stand his ground.
This moose is safe for one more day,
But patient wolves will have their way

In the Forests of the Great North Woods.

Yearling male moose

AT NIGHT IN THE GREAT NORTH WOODS ...

Snatched up by a raccoon's paws,

Crayfish crunch in toothy jaws.

A careless vole, a sudden squeal—

Great horned owl grabs his meal.

North American raccoon; northern crayfish

Star-nosed mole has broken ground
To take a peek, to look around.

Star-nosed mole; bluebead lily

Barn owl plummets. A frantic *squeak*

Marks a different meal in a different beak.

Barn owl; meadow vole

Red fox slinking from his den
With hopes of turkeys in the glen.

A white-tailed deer, her spotted fawn,
Bedded down, await the dawn

At Night in the Great North Woods.

Red fox

A thousand lakes, a thousand streams,
A lifetime's worth of nature's dreams.
Spruce grouse beating on their chests,
Wood ducks squatting on their nests.

Spruce grouse; Canadian bunchberry

Rousing duets from the wren and the lark,
Woodpeckers hammer on tamarack bark.
Through rich golden meadows, coyotes parade,
As rabbits and hares hunker down in the shade.

Pileated woodpecker on a tamarack

Porcupines clamber up jack pine trunks,
Below them are chipmunks and snuffling skunks.
Black bears are lumbering, ravens are gliding,
Beavers are building, and otters are sliding...

To Life in the Great North Woods.

North American porcupine